IMAGES
of England

POOLE
THE SECOND SELECTION

All the fun of the fair on The Quay, organized by Poole Round Table, on the day of the Fishermen's Regatta in 1983. Fun evenings with fireworks became a popular regular attraction on Thursdays during July and August from 1998. On Tuesdays The Quay became a bikers' haven.

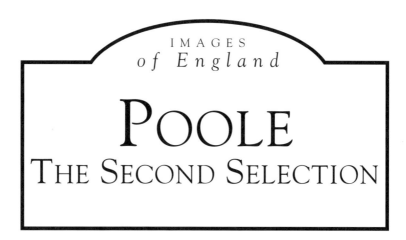

IMAGES
of England

POOLE
THE SECOND SELECTION

Compiled by
Ian Andrews and Frank Henson

TEMPUS

First published 2000
Copyright © Ian Andrews and Frank Henson, 2000

Tempus Publishing Limited
The Mill, Brimscombe Port,
Stroud, Gloucestershire, GL5 2QG

ISBN 0 7524 1624 3

Typesetting and origination by
Tempus Publishing Limited
Printed in Great Britain by
Midway Clark Printing, Wiltshire

Florrie Taylor and Leslie Poole, employees of Gould's newsagent in Towngate Street. Leslie Poole set up in business on his own in North Street in 1937.

Contents

Poole's links with Newfoundland started in the sixteenth century, when Poole fishermen exploited the rich supplies of cod on the Grand Banks. After providing Poole with great prosperity, the trade died in the nineteenth century, but in the 1980s the ties were renewed. Peter Coles (left), then Mayor, welcomed Newfoundland premier Brian Peckford to the Lester Room of the Mansion House in December 1982. They are photographed in front of a marble fireplace with an inlaid motif depicting dried salt cod.

Introduction

We are pleased to be able to respond to the requests for a further volume of archive pictures of Poole. After our last volume many people, good friends, came up to us saying, 'If only we had known you were looking for pictures. I have…', and then proceed to show us gems from their own family albums. As before we have eschewed, where possible, those already well known through public collections, those published as postcards or appearing in other books. Even so, sadly, we have still not been able to use all the photographs available to us. The quality of some of the old photographs used may not always be up to modern professional standards, but some of them are included here because they are rare views or we can tell real life stories behind them.

Public record offices and archives are often rich in photographs of streets and building exteriors or of major public events, but only in books like these can this basic framework of a town be clothed with pictures that tell the story of what it was really like for the man in the street to live, work and play in the town. Often these photographs do not paint a paradise, but bring out something of the spirit and show personalities of past times.

Many of the donors of these pictures had thought their photographs were only of interest to themselves or their families but by opening up their memorabilia to a wider public, they have in fact helped to recreate and record a way of life, occupations and some of the town's lost communities for all to share. We know the book will spark memories among the older generation and inform a younger audience of how the town has evolved over the last century.

To each and everyone who has helped us we are eternally grateful that in this new Millennium their treasures will add a human dimension to studies of Poole's recent history.

Ian Andrews and Frank Henson
Poole
December 1999

Acknowledgements

The late H. Ashley, G. Austin, R. Baker, Mrs J. Ballam, D. Barfoot, the late S.W. Batting, H. Beal, I. Brassfield, J. Buckby, Mrs L. Burrows, R. Cane, A. Carter, D. Cave, R. Clark, Mrs J. Clist, B. Coe, D. Colclough, E. Coleman, Mrs J. Crabb, C. Cruddas and Cobham plc, P.F.D. Davidson, Eldridge Pope & Co., G. Elsworth, T. Fancy, Mrs P. Froud, B.J. Galpin, Mrs C. Griffin, Hall & Woodhouse Ltd, P. Harvey, A.D. Hawkes, B. Hawkins, Mrs H. Henson, K. Hiscock, P. Hiscock, M. Hopkins, Mrs S. Hopkins, Mrs P. Howe, Canon Peter Huxham, Mrs J. Hunt, Mrs P. Jarvis (Poole Hospital Trust), K. Hiscock, A. Legg, B. Leverett, D. Lezso, R. King (Bourne Steel), Merck plc (B. Kettlewell), J. Milton, S. Moody, Mrs J. Morton, J. Oakley, D. Ould, Mrs C. Pearcy, Mrs C. Perry, N. Plumley, B. Poole, Poole Historical Trust (for pictures from the C.D. Barlow, Forsey, Bristowe and Swain collections), Poole Lifeboat House Museum, Poole Town FC Supporters Club, J. Pound, K. Prior, L. Ryall, Mrs A. Segall, P. Sharpe, T. Sherwood, Miss S. Sieger, B. Spinney, P. Swatman, R. Tolson, P. Toms, A.G. Yeatman (High Sheriff of Poole and Dorset 1999/2000) T&GWU (Poole Docks Branch), Mrs Tucker, Mrs D.E. Webster OBE, Miss D. White, G. Wills, Miss P. Wilnecker, F. Wretham (Mayor of Poole, 1999/2000).

For digital copying we are grateful for the services of Minuteman, Ashley Cross, Parkstone and for printing from negatives, Paul Williams of Bournemouth Road, Parkstone.

Where material is still in copyright we believe we have the permission of the owners to reproduce their material, but we would be glad to be advised if we have unwittingly infringed any person's rights or claims.

One
Poole Town
Football Club

The triumphant Poole Town team hold aloft their captain, Bill Burchett, *c.* 1950. They are celebrating a victory over Max Factors in the Bankes Senior Charity Cup at the Bournemouth Gasworks Sports Ground.

The Dorset Senior Cup Final between Poole Town and local rivals Longfleet St Mary's on 15 April 1905. There was so much excitement over this match in the town that the council gave permission for the game to be played in Poole Park, rather than their usual shared ground at Sterte.

The Mayor, Ald. R Simmonds, greets the referee before the kick off at the first match after the Second World War at Poole Stadium, against Wells City in the Western League, on 31 August 1946. Civic leaders took a great personal interest in the team's fortunes. Former MP Sir Mervyn Wheatley was proud to be the club president for many years.

Action from the FA Cup first round replay at Poole Stadium against Queens Park Rangers on 4 December 1946. After a heroic 2-2 draw at Loftus Road, Poole lost the replay 6-0 in front of a home crowd of 11,155.

The FA Cup first round replay, Poole Town *v.* Watford, at Poole Stadium in November 1962. Poole drew 2-2 away, but lost the replay 2-1. Poole Town was ejected from the stadium in 1994, after playing there for over sixty years, when the council approved plans for alterations that would not accommodate a football pitch.

Poole Town's international quartet, Wilf Mannion (Middlesborough and England), Stan Rickaby (West Bromwich Albion and England), Horace Cumner (Arsenal and Wales) and Stan Jones (Southampton and Wales), pictured in January 1956. Wilf Mannion was a magical inside forward and the golden boy of English football in the 1940s.

Wilf Mannion (centre) walks out to make his debut for Poole Town on 17 September 1955, in a Western League match against Frome. Wilf's international career came to an end after a serious knee injury in a match against Scotland at Wembley. He played for England twenty-six times.

Two
Events

An extraordinary picture of Branksome Home Guard on duty during the Second World War. This water-cooled machine gun is a typical example of local improvisation built to defend our country from the threatened invasion. The man on the left appears to have been the prototype for Corporal Jones, of *Dad's Army*!

The proclamation of King Edward VII at Britannia Road, Ashley Cross, Lower Parkstone, in January 1901. The councillors toured the borough, stopping at different locations to enable the mayor to read the Royal Warrant proclaiming the successor to Queen Victoria.

A mystery queue by the Guildhall in the early part of the twentieth century. The crowd is certainly a well-behaved one and they appear to be waiting patiently for something important but unfortunately we do not know what it was.

Princess Henry of Battenberg visited Poole in 1905 to promote the Young Women's Christian Association. After lunching at Weston House in High Street she proceeded to the Guildhall to be greeted by Mayoress Mrs Gwatkins. A detachment of the Royal Naval Reserve formed the Guard of Honour. The interior of the Guildhall was decorated as an English village street.

The opening of Poole Eisteddfod by Lady Cornelia Wimborne in the Amity Hall, High Street, in October 1908. The three-day event, a festival of arts and handicrafts, was organized by Skinner Street Congregational church and supported by most other churches in the borough.

The refreshment ladies at the Poole Eisteddfod, dressed in Japanese costume. Camp Coffee was advertised in the corners of the set.

High Street decorated for the Coronation of King George V in June 1911. The Amity Theatre is advertising a film of the Coronation for the following Saturday.

A great storm hit Poole on 25 April 1908 and up to two feet of snow fell on the town in two hours. Seemingly unaffected by the conditions this steam train carries on its journey.

The last Poole Carnival before First World War in June 1914. The Carnival Queen was Mrs H. Davis.

In 1908 a Norfolk man, Harry Bensley, undertook a $100,000 wager with American banker, John Pierpont Morgan. He undertook to live by selling postcards (like this one on his visit to Poole) and find a wife, while never removing the mask. The walk was abandoned at the start of the First World War, as Morgan feared he would not be able to pay out. He eventually paid Bensley $4,000 in compensation.

An exhibition stand promoting the Poole Harbour and District Improvement Society. The society was set up to assist and encourage the commercial development and general improvement of the port. This picture was in the society's 1921 handbook.

The Duke of York (later King George VI), in RAF uniform, laying the foundation stone of the Russell-Cotes Nautical School, on 8 May 1919. Among the guests on the rostrum are the Bishop of Salisbury, the Duke of Somerset and members of the Russell-Cotes family. The school closed in 1964.

The Mayoral Ball, 1932. There had been recent controversy in the town over the cost and location of the new municipal offices at Park Gates although, judging by the banner on the wall, these civic guests were expected to approve the council's actions.

The aftermath of the fire that gutted Kinson Pottery on 27 May 1957.

Sir Mervyn Wheatley (President of Poole Town FC), Sir Stanley Rous (Secretary of the FA), Fred Macey, Stan Pauley, Fred Hunt (Chairman of the Poole Town FC Supporters Club), the Mayor, Ald. Bill Cole and Bill Balance at the official opening of the new stand at Poole Stadium on 19 August 1961.

A Drum Head Service held in Poole Park to celebrate the Silver Jubilee of King George V on 5 May 1935. Five local bands took part and crowds assembled from all parts of the borough.

Poole tugboats, *Wendy Ann* and *Wendy Ann 2* at their berths near the bridge during the big freeze of 1963. Parts of the harbour were covered in ice for weeks; snow and ice bulldozed up from the roads was dumped on the beach at Branksome Chine.

The Hamworthy Lodge of the RAOB, popularly known as 'the Buffs', at the War Memorial by St Michael's church, Hamworthy, in the late 1920s. The rector, Revd Edward Hounslow, stands with his back to the camera. The post office in Blandford Road is just visible in the background.

Works manager Johnny Farrow (third from the left) joined the staff of Sharp Jones Pottery on Branksome Station, as they waited to board the special train hired to celebrate the centenary of the company.

Three
Schooldays

Snow White and the Seven Dwarves presented by the pupils of St Paul's High School, Alexandra Road, Parkstone, *c.* 1924. The Sisters of St Paul ran this convent school.

Broadstone School, Dunyeats Road, c. 1900. Sir Ivor Guest (later Lord Wimborne) and his wife provided this school for the then small village of Broadstone. The school bell was brought to England from Nineveh in Assyria by the famous archaeologist Sir Henry Layard and is thought to be over 3,000 years old.

Lady Cornelia Wimborne presenting the prizes at Canford School sports day. Canford School was formerly the home of the Wimborne family. The school opened in 1923.

Leonard Fancy in the uniform of Parkstone Grammar School, *c.* 1925. Boys wore short trousers until well into their teens in those days, something that would not go down well today, especially for the taller lads! Parkstone Grammar School and Poole Grammar School both became single-sex schools in 1937.

Martin Road School class orchestra in 1936. The teacher, Miss Delahuty, is well remembered by former pupils for her hat. Among the young musicians was Roland Clark, Mary McKenzie, Alan Yarwood, Ernest Voller, Barbara Conway and Margaret Randall. The conductor, Doreen Dorance, later became a professional singer.

Schoolchildren from Johnson Road, Oakdale, enjoy a street party to celebrate the Coronation of Queen Elizabeth II in June 1953. The party was held on land next to Oakdale Methodist church. In the background on the left is an old farmhouse in Old Wareham Road.

The Haynes School of Dancing float at the Poole Youth Carnival in 1957. Among the members on the tableau was Gordon Elsworth, who later, with his brother Ray, played in the Ambassadors dance band for thirty years. Twenty-six floats took part in the parade but disappointingly, it was reported, only £60 was collected in that year for the Poole Old Folks Christmas Parcel Fund, less than in previous years.

26

Children at a VE Day party in Lester (now Jolliffe) Avenue in 1945 to celebrate the end of the Second World War. The allotment gardens of the Poole Union (Workhouse), now the site of Longfleet School, are in the background. Frank Henson, one of the compilers of this book, is in the front of the picture, looking less than happy at having his picture taken!

Longfleet School country-dance team at the Dorset Schools' Country-Dance Festival held at Bovington Camp in 1957. Holding the school banner are Hilary Budge and Barbara Mizen.

The captains of the winning house receive the trophy at the Longfleet Junior School sports day in the 1960s. Among those watching are Mrs Reed, the headmistress, the vicar of St Mary's, Longfleet, Revd Kenneth Prior, and school manager Bernard Spinney with his wife.

The Pirates of Penzance, produced by the boys of Poole Grammar School in 1953. The musical director was Geoffrey Tristam, a master at the school and organist at Christchurch Priory. He often gave recitals on the radio. Do not be fooled by the rows of 'pretty girls' – they were all boys from the school!

Four

At Work

Poole 'dockies' unloading timber 'Up Sydnams'. Among the gang are Alf James, Fred Ball, Bill Neville, Jim Penney, Bert Irvin (the winchman), Charlie Kenway, Bill (Bougie) Davies, Jim Arnold and Len Phillips. Some of the workers are wearing protective shoulder pads.

Alice and Ivy, twin daughters of fishmonger Thomas Kearley, preparing to clean some fish in the yard of the family home, Bay Tree Cottage, Bay Tree Lane, in October 1910.

Fishermen's Dock, *c.* 1905. Net-drying stands were on both sides of the lifeboat house at this time. Despite strong protests from local residents the Harbour Commissioners have recently been granted permission to build a boat haven on the area with a toilet ship permanently moored alongside The Quay. According to one councillor the ship will be a tourist attraction!

Alfred Plumley (left) at his first job as deliveryman for G.W. Green, the local baker. In 1922 Mr Plumley bought his own milk business from Sam Whittle.

Ernest Rigler, who lived in Ivor Road, Hamworthy, pictured with piles of encaustic floor tiles at Carter's Tile Works (later Pilkingtons). Carter's floor tiles were a high quality product and were extensively used in buildings all over the country.

Staff of Dorset Iron Foundry, West Quay Road, in 1926. The business, one of many foundries in the town at one time, was started in 1880 and closed around 1960.

Some of the products of Dorset Iron Foundry at the 'Poole Can Make It' industrial exhibition, held in Poole Park in 1948. This was part of a local efforts to revitalize Poole's post-war economy.

The clay pits at Alder Road for Sharp Jones' Bourne Valley Pottery were acquired in 1886 and were originally connected to the main pottery by a horse-drawn railway. They are seen here around the turn of the twentieth century; the site is near the presenr Bloxworth Road.

Tom Fishlock of Bourne Valley (Sharp Jones) Pottery drives a car into one of the large stoneware sewerage pipes made by the company at Branksome.

The Bourne Valley (Sharp Jones) Pottery, founded in 1853, made mainly salt-glazed drainpipes. They had many outlets and markets for their products but among them was the developing new resort of Bournemouth, which was growing up next to Poole during the late nineteenth and early twentieth centuries.

Poole dock workers taking a well-earned break while working on The Quay. One of them is taking the opportunity to enjoy an ice cream from a vendor's barrow. Dock work was very hard and dirty, especially when there were coal boats to unload. W.B. Trimmer's fish store in the background is a reminder of the cod trade with Newfoundland.

In 1940/41 the British Power Boat Company (motto, 'Tradition, Enterprise, Craftsmanship') built a yard in West Quay Road, in double-quick time, to make wooden laminated MTBs to the design of Hubert Scott-Paine. The work was so urgent for the war effort that bad weather was no deterrent and thirty gunboats and launches were completed even before the factory was finished. British Drug Houses (BDH, later Merck) took over the premises after the war and the buildings were demolished in 1999.

Workers employed by J. Bolson and Sons preparing for the launch of a company pleasure boat. Jake Bolson started his first boat-building business at New Quay Road, Hamworthy, in 1931, expanding later into other premises at West Quay Road. The business closed in 1998 and Poole Harbour Commissioners leased the Hamworthy yard to Sunseekers International in 1999.

Toolmakers in the workshop of Chalwyn Lamps, Old Wareham Road. Chalwyn was a major manufacturer of hurricane lamps.

A magnificent silver teapot, presented to John Lawford, general manager of George and Harding Ltd, for his supervision of the restoration of Branksea Castle after the fire of 26 January 1896.

Workers in the West Quay Road premises of British Drug Houses in 1947. The recruitment of men into the Armed Forces during the war brought about many social changes at home, and women workers in factories remained a common sight even after peace was declared and the menfolk returned to 'civvy street'.

The press room at Humphris Engineering, West Quay Road. The company manufactured spanners and other pressed steel products, later expanding into the premises next door previously occupied by Corona, the soft drinks company. The factory closed in the late 1970s. The Ryvita Co., bombed out in Birmingham in the Second World War, moved into a factory at Old Wareham Road, originally built for Humphris Engineering.

Hamworthy Engineering, under Ingram Spencer, first operated on the Ham side of The Quay, but nowadays occupies large premises at Fleets Bridge. This interior view shows the set-up in the late 1960s, under Powell Duffryn ownership, before computer-controlled machine tools were the order of the day.

Construction of the long awaited Towngate Bridge, which got rid of the bottlenecks and traffic jams at the level crossings. On the right are the Victorian railway buildings. The Station Hotel is on the left. Safety regulations would prevent the public (and the photographer) from having such a close view of the work today.

Five

Pubs

The King's Arms on the corner of The Quay and High Street in 1927. Since the 1970s the pub has had two name changes; firstly to The Helmsman, which did have some nautical connection, but latterly to the Slurping Toad, a pub chain name foisted onto Poole by the brewery.

The most unusual pub sign in the Borough is probably at The Shah of Persia, Longfleet. The sign has four sides, with a different character from the writings of Omar Khayyam depicted on each side. These original 1932 paintings were by Francis Newbery, a noted artist living in Corfe Castle. The figures have been repainted several times, but in keeping with the original theme.

The Bull's Head in High Street in 1927. A corn merchant is on the corner of Prosperous Street. The Bermuda Triangle in Parr Street, Lower Parkstone, was also originally named the Bull's Head.

The London Hotel, High Street, was one of Poole's historic inns and the headquarters of the Reform Party in the 1830s. The premises were substantially altered in 1936 and renamed The Old Harry, after internal modification, in 1969.

The Rising Sun in Castle (Fish) Street. This seventeenth-century building was originally a hostelry comprising four other buildings and the inn. When this picture was taken Eldridge Pope were still calling their brews Dorchester Ales. The Rising Sun was demolished in 1960.

The Pure Drop, East Street. This was originally a private house, becoming a brewery and malt house in 1832. In this photograph from the 1920s a sack hoist to the loft is still in place.

The Star in West Street, opened around 1832, closed in 1956 when the New Star at Rossmore opened. The Star was previously called the Air Balloon and the Bricklayers' Arms.

The Harbour View, East Quay Road. Built in the 1830s, it was closed during the mid-1940s and used as a fish wholesaler's depot. The building was demolished in 1958 during the Old Town redevelopment.

The Bridge Inn, West Quay Road, so called because of its close proximity to Ham Bridge, was opened in 1886 and closed in 1968.

There were two public houses in Poole called the White Hart. One was in High Street and is now the site of Halfords. The White Hart in West Quay Road, pictured here, closed in 1956 and the buildings were used as a builder's yard and offices.

Railway stations frequently had a hotel built nearby and Poole station was no exception. The Station Hotel in Towngate Street was built in 1874 and demolished in the 1970s. The site is now occupied by an office block, Merchants' House. Notice that Strong's of Romsey, a rival brewer, have cheekily placed a poster on the wall to the left.

The George, Upper High Street, was originally called The George and Antelope. The old pub pictured here was demolished in 1927 and replaced by the present Inn. Mr R. Adams and his son, Ted, were landlords from 1919 until the early 1960s.

The Shah Of Persia, Fernside Road. There is an 1869 reference to a newly erected dwelling house and beer house on this site, occupied by Frederick Styring as tenant who bought and probably renovated the premises in June 1876. The original pub pictured here was demolished and replaced in 1931.

The Grasshopper, Bournemouth Road, built in 1873, is a pub that has reverted to its nickname. Seen here in 1927 as the Halfway Hotel, it was earlier commonly called the Grasshopper, as these tiny creatures were then abundant on the now developed heathland surrounding it.

The Woodman Hotel, Branksome. There have probably been licensed premises on this site since 1853. This building was demolished in 1968 and redeveloped as a ten-pin bowling alley with a new pub adjacent to it.

Six
Shopping

Mr H. Scott, proprietor of the Half Price Grocery Stores, and his staff at 59 High Street, close to Old Orchard, *c.* 1930. In 1935 there were twelve grocers' shops in High Street.

In 1906 John Lucas, who lived nearby in Longfleet Road, kept this small shop at the junction of Garland Road with Union Road (now St Mary's Road). He sold bread and groceries (including the inevitable Sunlight Soap and Fry's Cocoa) to his neighbours in the manner of so many other now long-gone corner stores. The premises have now been converted to domestic use.

Hall & Woodhouse's off-licence in Ashley Road, pictured in 1927, was one of many established in the 1890s. It is remembered in more recent years as the Edelweiss Restaurant and is now Bodycare, a thriving ladies' health and beauty salon – changes that reflect modern needs.

Marks & Spencer's window in High Street, *c.* 1935.

Alice Poole outside a family shop at 74 West Street. Miss Poole was the niece of Samuel and Isobel Poole, who owned the business from 1870 to 1918. Shops opened long hours, especially at weekends, as their customers often were not paid until late on Friday or on Saturday.

Leslie Poole outside his shop in North Street. Many of the goods he sold, including tobacco products, are well advertised on the wall of his shop. Small, family-run or one-man shops were a common feature of many side streets.

A 1921 advertisement for Butler & Son's two shops in High Street. The drapery store at 89 High Street was known to later generations as Bon Marché (now Yates's Wine Lodge). The hardware shop lasted until the 1950s when Newbery's furniture shop occupied the premises (now Burger King).

BUY YOUR PETROL at Butler's Pump IN NORTH ST.

THE PETROL goes straight from the pump to your tank, full measure every time ; no loss through spilling or evaporation ; no tins to pay for. First Quality only, in Pints, Quarts, ½ Galls and Galls.

Above
BUTLER & SONS'
DRAPERY DEPTS.
89 High Street, Poole

FOR
VALUE
—whether your shopping needs be personal Wearing Apparel, Furniture, Carpets, China and Glass, Household Hardware or Builders' Ironmongery — you cannot do better than buy at BUTLERS'. At both their establishments—89 & 134 High Street, you invariably get the VERY BEST OF QUALITY AT THE KEENEST POSSIBLE PRICE.

Above: BUTLER & SONS' HARDWARE SHOWROOMS, 134 High Street, Poole.

BUTLER & SONS
HIGH STREET ———————— POOLE
Branches at BOSCOMBE, WESTBOURNE, WINTON, WIMBORNE

J.G. Bailey, pictured here with his assistants, opened a butcher's shop at 53 High Street in 1910. The delivery boy, Harry Moody, was paid 4s a week. Wether mutton was the meat from castrated rams.

For forty years the business of S.H. Ould and Son was in Victoria Terrace, Ashley Road. This photograph was taken around 1891, soon after the shop opened as The Cash Stores.

This wider stretch of pavement at the upper end of High Street, seen around 1914, was known as The Promenade. George E. Fry, cycle and gramophone dealer (displaying a cycle on the roof), traded in a house converted to a shop on the immediate right, next to the Poole and Parkstone Co-op. Drum Druid, the former turnpike house (demolished *c.* 1935), obscures the George Hotel. An early AA sign hangs outside another shop, but only carts and bicycles are visible, as well as the elegant tram poles and the (single) track leading up Longfleet Road.

It is rare to find shop interiors on film. This is a corner shop which developed from a private house in Sandbanks Road, Whitecliff, originally known as Wilson's Alexandra House and later as Island View Stores. The view to Brownsea Island was lost because of development in the 1930s. It was Gane's when pictured here, after the Second World War, and is now Court Stores.

Bruce Forsyth signing autographs for fans when he opened a branch of Bourne Radio, electrical and record stores, in Ashley Road. The shop assistant on the right, Sandra Budge, was transferred from the Poole branch of the company to work in this new store.

Herbert J. Elcock soon after he took over the shop at Penn Hill in 1919. Note the glazed tiles alongside the shop, which still survive. Similar tiles on a nearby shop (formerly Vernon and Tear's) have now been given protection by a local listing.

Seven
Personalities

Mayor Cllr Mrs Doris Webster with Sheriff Cllr Peter Coles (right), and oil magnate Algy Cluff (left), who then owned Furzey Island (later sold to BP) laying a commemorative stone at the Quay Hotel in April 1980. The hotel was built by a local consortium led by Mrs Rachel Allenby and later sold to Mount Charlotte Hotels (Thistle).

Charles Van Raalte, then the popular owner of Branksea Island, addressing an election rally near the Ansty Arms. He made three unsuccessful attempts to win the East Dorset seat (which then included Poole) for the Conservatives, in 1902, 1904 and 1906. On the right is the first Longfleet Congregational church, later the Electric Cinema and, before its eventual demolition, Oswald Bailey's.

Winston Churchill (fourth from left), then a Liberal, opened the Branksome Liberal Club in 1910. He was related to the Guest family (Lord Wimborne), Lords of the Manor of Canford. He was later to become a Freeman of Poole in recognition of his role as wartime leader.

The late Miss Mary Llewellin, Poole's first lady mayor, twice mayor of Poole and the only Honorary Alderman so far created in Poole. She was a leader of the Guide movement in Dorset, and is pictured in the family home of Upton House. The house was later left to Poole Council, 'for public enjoyment', by her brother in his will.

Bill Harvell of Poole Wheelers, who rode for England in the Empire Games of 1930 and for Great Britain in the Olympic Games of 1932. He is seen here in road racing black tights; any sign of bare legs would have earned pre-war road racers immediate disqualification.

Popular entertainer Billy Cotton had a house in Panorama Road for over thirty years. He kept his motor launch, *Wakey-Wakey* (named after his famous catch phrase), in the harbour and often greeted boat trippers as they passed.

Mrs Burden, the landlady of the Port Mahon Castle public house during the Second World War. Like most pubs at the time there was always a warm welcome for servicemen. On the right is Harry Terry who is in BOAC uniform. He was a mail and cargo officer in the airline's Poole office. BOAC was formed in 1939 but put under military control during the war.

A sometimes fiery character, who collected all the civic honours Poole could bestow (Alderman, Mayor and Freeman of the Borough), millionaire Freddie Rowe OBE had an abiding interest in sport, chairing both Poole Sports Council and the South West Sports Council. He played cricket and was a racehorse owner. His firm, Cooper and Rowe, built many public buildings, including the Dolphin Swimming Poole. He died aged ninety in January 2000.

Mayor Bob Hann of Broadstone and Sheriff Jack Mears entertaining the longest standing and the most recent council tenants to tea in January 1969. Mrs Agnes Peaty and Mrs Lily Bishop, both of Jubilee Road, Upper Parkstone, had been tenants since 1920. The newest tenant, Mr Percy Stone, had moved in to a flat in South Road only two days previously.

Who has not been 'caught by the bridge'? Arthur Legg of Blandford Road, Hamworthy, took the opportunity to snap Bruce Forsyth in the early 1960s as he was held up in the queue of traffic waiting for Ham bridge to open.

Len Matchan was Labour parliamentary candidate for Poole in 1951 and a member of Poole Council. His business grew from a firm he created with Edward Webster making lipstick containers to become the Cope Allman business conglomerate. Being a millionaire he said socialism was a luxury he could afford. He later purchased the Channel Island of Jethou where he died in 1987.

Eight
Physical Jerks

The display team from Poole Parkstone Sea Training School (founded as Russell-Cotes Nautical School) smartly performing their routine for the school open day in 1955. The boys' families and invited guests are seated in the background. The team was of a very high standard and woe betide any boy who made a mistake!

Andy Sawyer of Poole Wheelers, the former Junior National Cyclo-Cross champion, competing in a race at Ham Common in the early 1970s. Unfortunately, because of a back injury Andy had to retire from cycling when he was eighteen. In the background is Rockley Sands holiday caravan park, developed by Alex Levy and George Stone, on land leased from the council.

R.P. Oakley, whose uncle Frederick gave the Town Cellars to Poole Council (the donation to take effect when there was no longer an Oakley living or working in the Borough) was a corn merchant. He was also a member of Poole Amateur Rowing Club and is seen at number two, taking part in the coxed fours, c. 1912.

Ted Sherwood of Parkstone, proudly wearing one of his many lightweight championship belts. He started boxing in the fairground boxing booths at Poole and had over 360 fights, winning most of them. He later became a Pentecostal preacher and taught a young Ian Paisley, who mentions Ted in his autobiography, the art of preaching.

Cycling and athletic events in Poole Park were very popular in the 1930s and '40s, events often attracting up to 10,000 spectators. The lady high jumper pictured here is competing bare-footed. In the background is Harold Cribb, a member of Poole Wheelers for over fifty years.

Poole Gymnastics Club in 1926/27. The gymnasium was attached to the library in Mount Street which is now part of Lagland Street.

The tug-of-war team from Pitwines taking the strain on the rope at the annual Southern Gas Sports held on the Alder Road Sports Ground.

Percy Baker, of Poole Park Bowling Club, was a bowling 'legend'. In his long reign as a top player he became the first man to win the English singles title four times. He also won the pairs twice and the triples once. His record of seven championships stood until 1952. He represented England in fourteen championships.

Members of Longfleet Congregational church tennis club at the club court in Longfleet Road. Jean Spinney, watching from the background (sporting an outrageous pair of sunglasses!) will be well remembered by former pupils of Oakdale Middle School as Mrs Hunt.

Poole Swimming Club members on the diving board at the open-air baths in Park Lake Road, *c.* 1930. The first Poole swimming baths were in the harbour at Baiter, where the foundations can still be seen today. Many boys from Poole Grammar School, when at Kingland Road, will remember swimming lessons in these cold water baths on cool spring days.

Nine
Proclaiming the Faith

Branksome Salvation Army Corps pictured in front of the stable doors in front of their old hall in Davis Road.

BOURNE VALLEY
FOR JESUS.

Great Invasion
ON
Saturday, Sunday and Monday
December 3rd, 4th and 5th,
LED ON BY

STAFF-CAPT. HOLLAND,
And a Host of Warriors.

BRASS BAND & TROOPS FROM POKESTOWN.

SATURDAY, December 3.	GREAT BOMBARDMENT & TERRIFIC BATTLE at 7 o'clock, followed by a MEETING at 8 o'clock. All are Welcome.
SUNDAY, December 4.	7 a.m.—Free Breakfast. 11 a.m.—Holiness unto the Lord. 3 p.m.—Free and Easy. 6-30 p.m.—Salvation for all.
MONDAY, December 5.	ALL ARE INVITED to hear the Saved BARMAN at 7 o'clock. All Meetings in Salvation

A Salvation Army poster of 1887. The organisation was very strong in the Branksome area and the promise of a free breakfast was a great attraction for many poorer families despite the early start. The 'saved barman' was a regular feature of the Salvation Army rallies.

St Clement's church, Newtown, *c.* 1910. The land through the gate on the left was known locally as the Vicar's Field. In 1934 a local lad playing with matches in the field accidentally set fire to the long grass and only the prompt action of the fire brigade saved the church from being damaged.

St Andrew's chapel (right) was attached to Parkstone Sea Training School (Russell-Cotes Nautical School). The pupils at this residential school wore naval uniform when out of the school. The school marching band often paraded through the streets and was one of the finest in the area.

St Mary's Roman Catholic church (also dedicated to the non-existent St Philomena) originally stood in West Quay Road, where the RNLI headquarters now stands. At the time of this photograph the shoreline, used for unloading timber, was opposite and the church had a clear view to Upton House, where the Doughty family, substantial benefactors to the church, lived.

In the woods of Chaddesley Glen, Canford Cliffs, is the Church of the Transfiguration. The first church, seen here, opened in 1911 and was built of timber and pebbledash, with a tin roof. The present church, consecrated in May 1965, was cleverly built around the older building, at a cost of £59,050. In 1999 the parishioners laid out a Millennium Garden.

A Longfleet Congregational church Sunday school parade passing Longfleet Restaurant (later Dolphin Hotel), c. 1935. In 1932 the Sunday school had 154 children and 32 officers and staff.

Ten
Transport

Mrs Helen Smee, her son Bobby, and daughter Sally, with neighbours of Cecil Road, Branksome, sitting in a veteran car belonging to Mrs Bannister of Pine (now Argyll) Road, in 1936. The car is an old one, probably from before 1903, and it doesn't appear capable of going very far - all the tyres are flat! In the back is the playground of Martin Road school.

The ferry between the Shipwrights Arms and the Custom House steps was the regular method of crossing between Ham and Poole for centuries, even after the first bridge was constructed in 1835. Even today, when the bridge is closed for maintenance, foot passengers can use a boat provided for their convenience although all other traffic has a long detour.

Ben Olliver was one of the many regular Ben Line coasters seen in Poole in the 1950s, when the firm of John Carter (Poole) Ltd was still operating on The Quay as ship owners and brokers.

Norman Plumley (left), with a young friend, on a wagon owned by his father's firm outside his home in West Butts Street. His mother is watching from the doorway.

A rare photograph taken on Brownsea Island during the the time of its ownership by the reclusive Mrs Bonham Christie. Bill Baker (right) was one of the few workers to remain on the island, leaving after the Second World War when he was employed by the RMYC at Sandbanks.

This car with a difference (the door was on the passenger side) was the gift of local businessman, Joe Huxham, to his Oxford undergraduate son, Peter, on his twenty-first birthday. With only one previous owner, the 1925 Doctor's Coupé Morris Cowley, seen here at Salterns House, had been in Poole since new. Peter became vicar of St Osmund's church, then team vicar of St Peter's, Parkstone, before moving to Taunton.

Reg Pound, with his nephew Jimmy Trickett, outside his home at Bowling Green Alley in 1937, on a 500cc Ascot Pullman belt-driven motor cycle. There were only seven of these machines manufactured.

Roger's Transport (Parkstone) Ltd owned one of the largest lorry fleets in the area. This picture was taken at the company's depot in Fancy Road in the 1960s. The workshops of Brixey Engineering, who were also specialists in crane hire, can be seen in the background.

An ARP ambulance in the Old Town during the Second World War. In the middle of the picture is Fred Kearley, who played football for Poole Town during the 1930s.

The name of the tug *Peter Joliffe*, seen off Ham side in the 1950s, recalls a famous sea captain from Poole who was awarded a gold medal in 1694 by William III for beating off a French privateer three times the size of his *Sea Adventurer* and beaching it in Lulworth Cove.

More recently the tug in use in the harbour was named *Wendy Ann*, operated by Harry Rose, and this was later joined by *Wendy Ann 2*. The tugs were taken over by Poole Harbour Commissioners.

The *George Jennings* was operated by South Western Pottery on the private line between Parkstone station and the company's works, seen in the background.

The Rossmore Bus, nicknamed the 'Rossmore Flyer', outside the terminus at Albert Road, Parkstone, in 1966. Owned by Miss Louie Foott (Mrs Dingwall), she originally ran a 'gypsy service' to Ashley Road from Rossmore Road for her Romany relatives, using a converted Model T Ford given to her by the Canadian Army after the First World War.

Poole, always considered a safer harbour than Southampton, was home for flying boat operations for the duration of the Second World War. After the war BOAC was anxious to resume long distance civilian routes from here. The nose of this silver painted Hythe class Sandringham taking off from the harbour clearly shows its recent former use: a gun turret is clearly visible.

Flight Refuelling, founded by visionary Sir Alan Cobham, in the 1930s, only came into its own after the Second World War. On 7 August 1949 this Gloster Meteor 3 could be seen over Poole being refuelled by a Lancaster, using the newly invented probe and drogue method. On this flight FR's test pilot, Paul Horridge, set up a world endurance record of 12hr 3min, during which his Meteor was refuelled ten times.

Eleven

Poole Lifeboats

The *Bassett Green* lifeboat was at Poole from 1962 to 1969. It was a Liverpool class boat and the first Poole lifeboat to be permanently moored outside the boathouse in Fisherman's Dock. While at Poole it was launched seventeen times, saving nine lives.

Arthur Brown, in his lifejacket, c. 1935. He was recruited for the lifeboat in 1933 as the signalman because of his knowledge of semaphore, learnt in the Indian Army. He served in the lifeboat for thirty years. Before radio was introduced the signalman had to contact the coastguard by semaphore using an Aldis lamp.

The Harmar lifeboat was stationed at Poole from 1910 to 1929. The boat was credited with saving sixty lives. In this picture it is seen meeting a Poole Harbour Board launch in open water outside the Haven.

Coxswain Albert Brown and members of the crew at the Lifeboat House practising putting on their lifejackets. Lifeboat crew need to dress speedily to get the boat into action as soon as possible in an emergency.

George Buckby, second coxswain and engineer in 1974/75, preparing to load the maroon used to signal the lifeboat crew into action. George joined his father-in-law, Arthur Brown, in the lifeboat in 1946 and served for twenty-nine years. When George's son, John, joined the crew in 1962 there were three generations of the family serving at the same time.

The *George Elmy*. This boat replaced the *Bassett Green* and was in Poole for just two years. During this time it was launched twelve times and saved three lives. Poole is now recognized as the busiest lifeboat station in the country.

Mayor of Poole, Cllr Elwyn Davies, and crew member John Buckby, leaping aboard the *Augustine Courtauld* in February 1969 when the boat was stationed at the PHYC marina at Lilliput. John Buckby joined the lifeboat in 1962 and was second coxswain from 1990 until he retired from the boat in 1998. The *Augustine Courtauld* was at Poole from 1974 to 1982.

Twelve

Gone Without Trace

The old gasworks on East Quay, *c.* 1910. The works provided gas for Poole and the surrounding area until Pitwines opened in 1925. The Harbour View public house can just be seen on the right.

The Station Hotel near the railway crossing in Towngate Street. The wooden hut on the left housed the gatekeeper's equipment for operating the crossing gate.

Houses on the corner of Lagland Street and Strand Street being demolished during the redevelopment of the Old Town in January 1959. The Swan public house (later the Flying Boat and now Murphy's) was popularly nicknamed the 'Mucky Duck' and can just be seen on the right.

Belben's Steam Mill on The Quay was destroyed by enemy action during the war. An office block for Christopher Hill Ltd, later used by the Harbour Commissioners, was built on the site.

Eric Coleman, now living in Oakdale, standing outside the house in Hill Street where he was born, shortly before it was demolished in 1966. The site is now a multi-storey carpark. In the background is the air-raid siren that was situated in the council depot (formerly the fire station) in King Street.

The Powder House was built at Baiter in 1775, using stone from the old Quay, to store gunpowder. All ships had to store explosives they were carrying here during their stay in port to avoid the risk of explosion on the Quays. This law was in force as recently as the Second World War. This interesting relic, despite local campaigns to preserve it, was demolished and only some unmarked foundations of the building are left today.

Denby Lodge, Breakheart Lane (now known as Fernside Road). This house was built in 1884 for Thomas Cox, a Poole merchant by day and poet by night, and was a bijou residence, with stables and over five acres of ground, extending a third of the length of Lester Road (now Jolliffe Road). Later Denby Lodge was the home of the popular Perman School of Dancing. The house was demolished in 1982.

Upper High Street in 1958. Two-way traffic here was already causing chaos at peak times. All of these buildings were demolished for the new shopping complexes.

Looking along Wimborne Road towards the fire station in 1958. Barclays DCO headquarters, (as it was when built), was moved from the City of London and now dominates the scene.

The Sharp Jones Pottery at Bourne Valley (later Redland Pipes) was a considerable landmark, standing at the junction of the routes to Bournemouth from Upper and Lower Parkstone. It is still known as Pottery Junction by many bus users. The Branksome Retail Centre now occupies the site.

Thirteen

Services

An aerial view of the landmark Poole Generating Station, built in 1947 after consultation over its design with the Royal Fine Arts Commission. Demolished in 1993, it was originally coal-fired but was later converted to oil. In both cases the fuel was delivered by sea and required the Hamworthy Bridge to be lifted.

Bournemouth and West Hampshire Water's works at Alderney, including sports facilities, c. 1955. Up to 1888 a thousand customers in Bournemouth and eastern Poole had to put up with discoloured peaty Bourne Stream water, pumped via a reservoir at Alder Road/Ashley Road. Better quality water, extracted from the River Stour at Longham and stored in a new reservoir and filtered at Alderney, then became available.

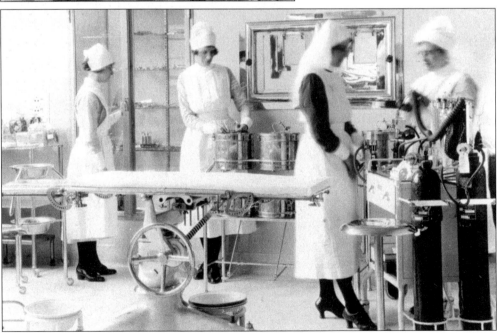

A view we don't often see (or perhaps wish to see!): the interior of the then well-equipped operating theatre in Poole (Cornelia) Hospital, which was the state of the art for its day, probably during the 1930s. The hospital has always been well supported by a League of Friends, who have donated much equipment over the years, often the result of annual fairs in Poole Park.

The office block of Pitwines gas plant in Green Road in 1939, soon after it was built. The building also housed the drawing office and laboratories. Houses in Green Road can be seen on the left.

On a Sunday soon after his inauguration the mayor gives thanks in a service at the Civic Church (St James'), conducted by his chaplain. Many of the town's organizations, some uniformed, accompany him to and from the Guildhall in procession, along with a band. This ceremony of 1955 was in honour of Mayor Cllr Charles E. Stokes. Cllr Arthur Lloyd Allen was Sheriff.

Many wells in the Old Town were below sea level and did not produce potable water. Tatnam Well, on higher ground, was the main water supply from the sixteenth to the nineteenth centuries. During the twentieth century the well was a favourite place for local children to collect tadpoles. A campaign to preserve the historic site was unsuccessful and the well was filled in for the development of Well Lane.

Public pumps were located near The Quay and at Ansty Arms in upper High Street, as well as in the heart of the Old Town, pictured here. They remained part of the street scene, visible in many old photographs, until redevelopment took place and they were removed to the museum.

Fourteen
Around the Borough

Enthusiastic crowds cheered a Southern Roadways lorry as it crossed the new Ham bridge, built by Cleveland Bridge Co. and opened on 9 March 1927. The lorry was loaded with coal to prove the strength of the structure. Seventy years later the bridge mechanism is bearing much heavier loads than this. In 1998 the government rejected imaginative plans for a replacement bridge over Holes Bay.

A nineteenth-century etching of 'the harbour within', Backwater Channel, above the bridge and leading to Holes Bay. The view, from Hamworthy, features St James' church and shows extensive use of the waterfront on West Quay Road, where many timber yards were situated.

An aerial view of the second Ham Bridge, *c.* 1920. Sydenham's timber yard and wharf is in the middle of the picture, with Carter's tile works on the right. The town's first railway station was at Hamworthy and is visible at the bottom left.

Holes Bay and the start of the construction of Holes Bay Road. Properties that had been on the waterside in Sterte Esplanade now became sandwiched between the railway and a major road.

Carters Pottery at Hamworthy is still remembered in the street name Carters Avenue. The pottery was run together with Kinson Pottery by William, son of Jesse Carter of Poole Pottery fame, and later by William's son, Ald. Herbert Spencer Carter OBE. The claypits at Hamworthy provided raw material for making bricks which were despatched, via a private railway siding to Hamworthy Junction, to all parts of the country.

Boatyards at Lake, Hamworthy, in the 1930s. Poole has always been an important centre for boat-building and the activities of boat owners have been important to the local economy. Today Sunseekers International and several other smaller boat builders continue the tradition of building first-class craft in the town.

Lord Rockley, who owned Ham Common (largely occupied by the Admiralty), relinquished his beach hut and sold his land to the council in 1956. Rockley Sands Ltd (Alex Levy and George Stone) carried out the development on lease of a leading caravan holiday camp by 1960, including the Palladium and a supermarket. Although visible from Purbeck it is hidden from the view of Poole residents.

The Drawing Room of Upton House while in the occupation of the Llewellin family, showing caryatids supporting a fireplace reputed to have been made for a Napoleonic palace. During the Second World War matters of great national importance were discussed here as Jay Llewellin served successively as Minister of Aircraft Production and Minister for Food. He was the last Governor-General of Rhodesia before independence.

Broadstone did not become part of the Borough until 1933. In 1906, when this photograph was taken, it was still a rural village. The view, taken from the hairpin bend on the Higher Blandford Road at Widworthy looking towards Broadstone station (then known as Poole Junction), clearly bears this out.

Ashington Mission church was originally a tin rest hut built for workmen constructing the Somerset & Dorset Railway. It was later converted to a church of the Canford Magna Parish and the bell cupola added. The church had room for about sixty worshippers and was only closed in the 1990s.

Canford Magna, *c.* 1910. This fine building was the home of Lord Wimborne who owned extensive land in the Borough and was a noted benefactor to the town. The house was built in the Gothic style in about 1850 and most of a former manor was demolished for the new building.

Stanley Green Lane, Oakdale (now Vicarage Road) in the 1920s. Oakdale was part of the Longfleet Parish and the Longfleet vicarage was situated near this part of the road. A vicarage was later provided next to St Mary's church.

The junction of Wimborne Road and Darbys Lane, *c*. 1925. Oakdale post office is in the middle of the picture and the school can just be seen in the background.

Hatch Pond in 1973. Most of this area has now been developed for housing and light industry. The pond has been stocked with fish and leased to a local angling club.

Constructing the Old Wareham Road in 1958. The MOD Experimental Establishment (MEXE), in co-operation with Rotary Hoes of Essex, used the construction of this road as a trial for a rapid road-making technique, laying up to 14ft a minute. The ground on the right now leads to the Tower Park complex.

Charles Trent's car scrap yard in about 1940. Michael Wills of Oakdale enjoys himself playing on the old car bodies but is being very careful to keep his clothes clean!

Ringwood Road looking towards Alderney in 1934. Charles Trent, car breakers, now occupy the land on the left of the picture.

The Alderney Brickworks (Dorset Brick and Tile Co.), had a prominent chimney to their kiln. The works flourished between 1919 and 1957 on a heathland site in Broom Road at Mannings Heath and was later acquired by British Drug Houses (BDH) for their offices and chemical store.

Gas holders at the Bourne Valley Gas Works in the 1930s. The ground, at Guest Avenue in the front, was developed for housing in the 1960s.

Laying a 14in gas main near Wallisdown cross-roads in May 1962. It wasn't busy enough then to warrant the later plea for a relief road.

Alder Road, Branksome, in 1930, before the gasworks sports ground was developed on the right. The area was low lying and over 52,000 cubic yards of soil were dug out of an overlooking hill to level the ground. The sports ground was opened in 1932 and eventually developed for housing in the 1960s after the council decided not to buy the ground.

Pineland Laundry on the corner of Bournemouth Road and Alder Road, Branksome. The original laundry was destroyed in an air raid in April 1941. This site, and Sharp Jones Pottery next door, now form Branksome Retail Centre.

Ashley Road, Branksome. The buildings on the left are to house the new Branksome Library.

The top end of Uppleby Road before it was made up. On the left were Turner's nurseries, in whose buildings a number of old cars were housed. The land is now public open space.

The Retreat Public House and adjoining Parkstone bus depot, now redeveloped as the Safeway supermarket.

This aerial photograph of Branksome Dene Chine in around 1935 shows the Chine Café erected above the beach on the site of the old Coastguard Cottages.

In 1895 the usual approach along the Avenue to the beach at Branksome Chine was on foot or by carriage.

By 1920 provision of a parking place for motor and other carriages had firmly established Branksome Chine as a tourist destination. A former thatched kiosk for refreshments had been replaced and Poole Corporation began to plan a modern bathing station. The cliff on the right was levelled and the sand transported to form Branksome Recreation Ground.

An aerial photograph from 1935 of the Cliff Drive area of Canford Cliffs.

Canford Cliffs Hotel at Canford Cliffs Chine (formerly Sugar Loaf or Smugglers' Chine) had a mock Martello Tower in its grounds as a smoking room. It was destroyed following an air raid in 1941 when there was insufficient water to extinguish the ensuing fires. The former stables are now the Nightjar pub and houses and flats now occupy the site. Former landlord Jimmy Cooper was well known for his showbiz connections.

Sandbanks, *c.* 1905. The highest dune on the peninsula, over 70ft high, was called High Horse Manger. Canford Estates offered Sandbanks to the Borough in 1895 and the mayor and some councillors expressed a wish to retain it as open space, but the first building plots were sold in 1896.

Sandbanks in the 1920s, showing the first café (which was only demolished and replaced in 1985), and a few wooden beach huts. In 1918, thirty beach hut plots were let for £2 10s 0d each.

THE HAVEN HOTEL

POSTAL & TELEGRAPHIC ADDRESS. "HAVEN HOTEL, POOLE."

PARKSTONE-ON-SEA.

Proprietor, W. H. Witherington. Late Manager, Bucklands Hotel. and Challis's Royal Hotel, LONDON, W.

In an advertisement for the Haven Hotel in *The Queen* magazine in 1896, Sandbanks was described as 'a tongue of land, a narrow strip so narrow in winter that the waves almost dash away the sand dunes, where gorse struggles to grow among the snow white silvery sand.' Along it were coastguard cottages, one house and the comfortable Haven Hotel. 'After we have been living at high pressure, rest we must have, and a pause is necessary to re-oil the engine.'

A ferry service between Sandbanks and Shell Bay operated for centuries, long before there was a chain ferry. The pier seen here was built in 1898. It is noticeable that more harbour mud is exposed than is usual today. The Haven Hotel, showing the masts used by Marconi for his experiments in transmitting wireless signals long distances over water, is in the background.

When Branksea Island was owned by the Van Raalte family in the early twentieth century it became one of the centres of Society life, and the gardens around the castle were much admired features. The head gardener, Thomas Pool, was sent to Kew Gardens to get ideas for the designs and the herbaceous border, pictured here, was one of the features he laid out.

A view in 1935 of the Shore Road/Banks Road area. The direct line of Chaddesley Glen was too steep for traffic and Haven Road was constructed to ease the gradient. In the midst of the trees the roof of the old Church of the Transfiguration can be seen.

Poole Harbour has always been a rich source of bait for anglers; rag and lugworms, razor fish and slipper limpets have always been abundant in the mud banks around the shore. These bait diggers at Sandbanks, pictured here by the late Harry Ashley of the *Evening Echo* in November 1974, are probably after lugworms.

In 1947, after wartime use as the BOAC and flying boat headquarters, Poole Harbour Yacht Club was opened at Lilliput (now Salterns Hotel and Marina). To create a sea wall, the former wartime Mulberry Harbour pontoons were reused.

An aerial view of George Jennings (South Western) Pottery taken in 1937. The pottery is in the middle of the picture with Sherry and Haycock timber merchants on the right. The area was developed for housing in the 1970s.

Captain Kimberley's Blue Lagoon (later owned by Ald. G. Bravery) was a private venture built in 1934 for boating, with a club house and a modern swimming pool. His daughter, Pauline, was the representative for the Royal Life Saving Society and by 1935, when this photograph was taken, Poole's first lifeguard corps, who patrolled Branksome Chine beach at weekends and trained at Blue Lagoon, had been established.

A bend in Sandbanks Road, between Elms Close and Elms Avenue, photographed by F. Cathery in the early 1900s.

The builder's plan for Park Estate is seen in this aerial shot dating from 1920. The origin of the street name Twemlow Avenue has eluded all researchers. Island Road was later renumbered in Orchard Avenue to avoid confusion with Highland Road by emergency services. A resident recalls a light plane from Wallisdown landing where Sherwood Avenue now stands.

Parkstone Motor and Cycle Co. (its original title) started life in Parr Street and in 1930 moved to a former house, Laurel Bank, in Station Road. Leslie G. Adams supplied many Austin and other cars to local motorists. The garage relocated to Cabot Lane in 1985 and became Diamond Motors. Homelake House now occupies the Station Road site.

Springfield House, Parkstone, was built for William Pearce, the owner of Poole Foundry. During the First World War it was used as a convalescent home for army officers. Sitting on the pillar second from the left is Wilfred Ould, whose family owned a general stores in Ashley Road. The house was later used as part of the Dorchester School.

Traffic in the 1920s, when this photograph of Castle Hill, Bournemouth Road, Parkstone, was taken, was notably lighter than it is today.

The Lion Coffee Tavern on the corner of Churchill Road and Ashley Road (later the Co-op and now a Hogshead pub). Many refreshing drinks are advertised on the notices outside the premises, which also gave a special welcome to cyclists. Judging by the prominent tobacco advertisements there would have been no restriction on smoking inside.

The view from Constitution Hill towards Longfleet in about 1905. Longfleet at this time was still a very rural area with only a few farm buildings and terraced houses, close to St Mary's church. The plot where the Shah of Persia pub now stands was sold in 1815 for £10. The isolation hospital at Baiter can just be seen in the background.

Poole Park was laid out in 1889 with a bandstand and horse chestnut trees lining the drives, and is seen here in 1905. Poole Silver Band were intermittently paid a grant to play there on Sundays. Current plans for Poole Park propose a new bandstand; one can only hope the council remembers to budget for a band to play here.

This engraving, made by Phillip Brannon of Southampton, illustrated the earliest guide book to Poole, published in 1857.

Poole Parks Department, under Ernest Gale, took a lot of pride in its three dimensional summer displays in Poole Park. This is the 1964 arrangement.

The construction of the Nurses' Home in the hospital grounds in 1966. At that time Pitwines gasworks was still belching out thick black smoke over the Old Town, as can be seen in the background of the picture.

Poole council house tenants pass the George Hotel in 1958, on their way to the Municipal Buildings at the Civic Centre to give voice to their protests on a recent rise in the rents. Despite strong emotions generated by the protest, the tenants appear to be giving the lone policeman on duty no worries as they continue their march.

The winding-up parade of the Second World War Fire Guard passes the saluting base in High Street by the United Reform church. The wartime signs pointing to public air raid shelters in Chapel Lane are still in place. The bus route from Hamworthy ran up High Street, as the bus stop on the right shows.

The George Hotel on 5 February 1935. Pedestrians at this time could cross the road after only a quick glance for any oncoming traffic. Many of these businesses still occupied the same premises when the area was redeveloped over thirty years later.

The tram terminus at Towngate Street, c. 1910. Dean's garden shop (Anthony's) was on the same premises until the 1970s, although the name changed later to Heather's. On the right were Poole Conservative Club and Shaftesbury Hall, demolished in 1963 when the club moved to the Lintlaw Lodge in Wimborne Road.

The Mayor, Cllr W.J. Stickland, unveils a commemorative plaque in May 1938 on the site of the Guildhall Prison in Castle Street, where the Revd John Wesley (grandfather of John and Charles Wesley), Poole's first Independent Minister, was imprisoned for six months in 1662. The plaque was later resited on the wall of Rank Hovis McDougall's new Agrarian House (now Raglan Housing Association's Wright House) in Castle Street in 1965.

Well-known Poole raconteur, George Blake, in Strand Street, during the 1980s, holding a wooden pile that was used to support The Quay over 400 years ago. Strand Street was once the shore line and The Quay has been extended over the centuries to reach deeper water. The piles were discovered when workers were repairing the foundations of an old building.

The Quay at its junction with High Street in 1926. The *Frome* tugboat had been used by Pike Bros to haul barges loaded with clay from Ridge since 1844. The Model T Ford (in black of course) was first produced in 1908 and ceased production in 1927. On the right grain sacks are being slid down from the upper floors of Oakley's Store which is now the Warehouse Restaurant.

Kennedy's slabbing workshop on The Quay made tiled fireplaces. Among the employees in the 1950s were Poole Town FC stalwart, Ted Kerslake and Dorset football referee, Sib Hibbs, who was a linesman for the 1958 FA Cup Final. The workshop moved to Nuffield Industrial Estate in the late 1960s, but was soon closed down. Purbeck Pottery showrooms now occupy The Quay site.

The first plaques marking historic sites in Poole were erected in the 1920s. The one on Burden's premises (now demolished) on The Quay marked the arrival of ex-King Charles X of France with his retinue in 1830. After a night at the Antelope Inn, he made his way to the sanctuary offered by the Weld family at Lulworth Castle.

Poole Regatta in the early 1950s. Large crowds could always be expected to watch the activities on the water at this important event in the town's calendar. In this picture a war-time Nissen hut can be seen in the top left-hand corner of the picture.

There is no precise record of when the J.T. Sydenham Timber Co. Ltd started in Poole, but by the time of the construction of the second Ham Bridge in 1884, when this picture was taken, the yard and mill were well established. They had a private siding to the railway and used horse-drawn wagons.

This aerial photograph covers the whole of the Old Town area of Poole and the docks, and was taken when the Truckline service to Cherbourg was inaugurated in 1974. The docks have since been expanded by further land reclamation, which has allowed a greater volume of trade between Poole and its twinning partner in France and elsewhere.

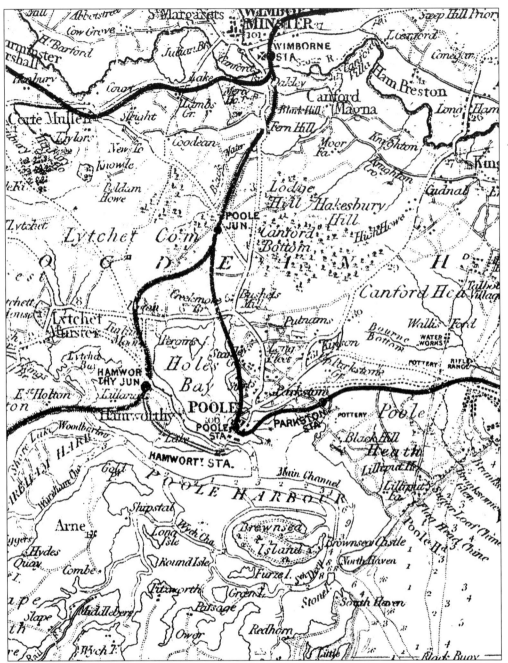

Poole has always been an interesting excursion destination for visitors from Bournemouth. This is an extract from a Hankinson map of 1876 prepared for such visitors and shows some interesting Poole features of the time including a rifle range at Branksome.